The Journal to Unlocking Your Freedom:

Overcoming Your Abortion

The Journal to Unlocking Your Freedom:

Overcoming Your Abortion

Kasandral Wells

J. Kenkade
PUBLISHING®
Little Rock, Arkansas

The Journal to Unlocking Your Freedom: Overcoming Your Abortion

J. Kenkade Publishing
6104 Forbing Rd
Little Rock, AR 72209
www.jkenkadepublishing.com

J. Kenkade Publishing is a registered trademark.

Printed in the United States of America
ISBN 978-1-944486-56-3

Acknowledgments

I would like to thank our Most High for giving me the courage and wisdom to write this life-changing Journal.

Thank you to Jordan and Ashston, my handsome sons, for being my strength. I also would like to thank my parents, Ruthie and Isaiah Wells, Sr. I would like to say a special thank you to my sister Karen and her husband Derrick. Also, thank you to my sister Lola along with my brothers, Isaiah Jr, Isaac, Chris, and Chane and to a host of family and friends.

Introduction

The purpose of this Journal is to help us face our hidden secrets of our abortion(s). My journey through my abortions was very difficult until I realized that I needed to face my hidden past. Facing my hidden past by writing and expressing through testimonies enabled me to overcome my actions of having an abortion bit by bit. Therefore, I want to share with you so that you can experience the same freedom.

And (they) overcame him by the blood of the Lamb
and the word of their testimony; and they
loved not their own unto the death.
Revelation 12:11

Ninety-nine percent of these questions I had to face. The reality of facing these questions was very hard because it meant rooting up my past. I had many tears, fear, guilt, shame, anger, jealousy and regrets. Many questions arose within me, and many of them I had no answers to. Writing and facing my story has helped me to overcome many challenges within my soul, although, I had to learn to press toward the mark of a higher call in the Most High.

Before I formed Thee (you) in the belly I knew thee:
and Before you camest forth out of the womb I sanctified thee,
and I ordained thee a prophet unto the nations.
Jeremiah 1:5

I, ______________________________ had an abortion(s).
(name)

Prayer

Yah (God), The Most High, I acknowledge that you are Yah. You are Yah of creation. You are Elohim. You are Yah of the Universe. Thank you for helping me to forgive myself. You are merciful and gracious. I thank you for healing and delivering me from every heaviness that was attached to the abortion(s). I accept your forgiveness into my heart. I will live to my full potential that you ordain for me. I will help others to walk into their purpose, to let them know that we do serve a true and living Yah. You are faithful, forgiving, and full of hope, joy, and peace. Abba (Father) thank you for forgiving me this day and for taking the spirit of death (abortion) and giving me the spirit of life (freedom). I love and bless your Holy Name. Amen. Shalom.

What was your experience before the abortion(s)?

How many weeks or months along were you when the abortion(s) was performed?

Did you have the abortion(s) due to lack of income?

Did you have support before and after your abortion(s)? Explain.

How did you pay for the abortion(s) or who helped contribute to the procedure(s)?

What age did you have your abortion(s)?

What type of abortion(s) did you have? Medication Abortion, Abortion Pill, Surgical Abortion, Aspiration or Suction?

Did you have a Sonography (ultrasound) before the abortion(s)?

If a Sonography was performed, do you believe you would have had the abortion(s)? Explain.

What was your experience at the abortion clinic?

What was the location of the abortion clinic?

What was the time and year of the abortion(s)?

Were you forced to have an abortion(s)? If so, by whom? Do you forgive him or her? Explain.

Do you feel you received proper counseling prior to the abortion procedure(s)?

How many abortions have you experienced?

Did you follow-up after your abortion(s)? Explain.

What was the hardest fear you faced before, during, and after your abortion procedure(s)?

Did you have a full or partial abortion(s)? Was the abortion(s) due to rape? Explain.

Was your abortion(s) due to an extramarital affair? Explain.

Did you tell your partner or will you tell your partner about the abortion? Explain. If not, why have you kept the abortion(s) a secret?

Have you thought of or tried suicide? Explain.

Did you or anyone else harm you mentally or physically because of the abortion(s)?

Do you have self-hate due to the abortion(s)? Explain.

Did you experience shame or guilt after your abortion(s)? Explain.

What health risks have you experienced after the abortion(s)?

Have you experienced any psychological effects after the abortion(s)? Explain.

Have you experienced depression after the abortion(s)? Explain.

Did you experience any regrets after the abortion(s)? Explain.

Did you pick up any habits after your abortion(s) such as sex, drugs, or alcohol?

Have you contracted any sexually transmitted disease(s)? Explain.

What side effects have you experienced after the abortion(s)? Explain.

Do you consider yourself as a murderer? Explain?

Are you married?

Do you have children?

Are you in a relationship?

Are you and the father of the aborted child in a relationship? Explain.

Are you in a stable location or have you moved from place to place? Explain.

Does your partner know about the abortion(s)? Explain. Did the abortion(s) affect your relationship(s)? Explain.

If you would have kept the baby, do you think you and your partner would still be together? Explain.

Was your abortion(s) with the same partner or different partners? Are you the only person in your family that has experienced an abortion(s)? Explain.

Did your mother or father have an abortion(s)? Does she/he talk about the experience? How did you find out?

Were you able to conceive after the abortion(s)? Explain.

Have you experienced miscarriages after the abortion(s)?

What health problems have you experienced after the abortion(s)? Explain.

How did you feel after the abortion(s)? Explain.

From a male perspective, did you encourage your partner to have an abortion(s)? Do you have regrets? Explain.

As a teenager, were you forced to have an abortion? By whom?

How was your experience? Do you have resentment? Explain.

How many people knew about your abortion? Explain.

Have you ever encouraged an individual to have an abortion? Do you regret it? Explain.

Was the abortion what you expected? Was it easier or harder?

What have you learned from the abortion(s)?

Have you heard a baby's cry after your abortion(s)? How long? What are your thoughts?

Has death taken place in your family because of an abortion(s)? Explain.

Do you trust yourself with children? Meaning, do you feel as though you don't have the ability to care for children?

Do you feel worthy to be a mother or a father after the abortion(s)?

Do you believe in yourself after the abortion(s)? Explain.

What is your career? Have you surrounded your career around babies or children? If so, why?

Would you share your experience with others or will you keep your experience to yourself? Explain.

Would you encourage others not to have an abortion(s) or would you let the person make their own decision? Explain.

Do you wish you would have had the baby adopted into a good family instead of having the abortion(s)?

Did you seek professional help (counseling) or did you take part in a deliverance class? If so, how did you receive your deliverance?

Have you forgiven yourself? Explain.

Everyone has a story. Has this journal helped you face your deepest secret(s)? Explain.

If your child or children were alive today what would you name him or her?

Do you feel your abortion(s) have affected the children you now have? Explain.

How would you base your life after your abortion(s)? Explain.

Was birth control part of your lifestyle before your abortion(s)? Explain.

Did you have complications during your abortion procedure(s)? Explain.

Were you able to use tampons after your abortion(s)? Explain.

Were you able to return back to work after your procedure or how long were you away from work? Explain.

How soon after your abortion did you return to your sexual activity? Explain.

Were you able to pay or take your medication after your abortion(s)? Explain.

Did you have a Dilation and Curettage (D&C) procedure? Explain.

Do they allow abortions in the country or state where you live? Explain.

Have you ever taken the morning after pill? Explain.

Reflections

What is your favorite color?

What is your favorite movie?

What is your heart's desire?

What are your hobbies?

Did something tragic happen to you that broke your heart before the abortion(s)?

What is your father's name?

____

What is your mother's name?

____

Do you have a relationship with your parents?

____
____
____
____
____
____
____
____
____
____
____
____
____
____
____
____
____
____

Do you have a relationship with your grandparents?

Do you have siblings? Do you have a relationship with your siblings?

Do you have a mentor?

Do you have a support team?

Did you have a good childhood?

Did you have an imaginary friend in your childhood?

Did or do you feel rejected?

Were you abandoned as a child?

What is your passion?

Are you a joyful or sad person?

Who are you as a person?

What is your purpose in life?

Are you a mother or a father?

Are you a friend?

Are you a kind or an evil person?

Do you want a child or children?

Are you happy?

What is the worst thing you've ever done?

What is the best thing you've done?

Do you like short or long hair?

Are you in your dream profession?

What's your dream car?

What's your dream vacation?

Did you marry for the purpose of convenience?

Are you controlling?

Are you teachable?

What's a good adventure story from your childhood?

Have you ever been in love?

Are you healthy?

Are you an alcoholic?

Do you exercise?

Are you a selfish person or do you find yourself pleasing people?

References

King James Bible
Bible Study Tools

Prayers

Lord forgive me for taking your grace, love, my life,
and the life of my child(ren) I aborted for granted.
Thank you for being Yah of grace, love, and life.

Lord thank you for covering me under your mighty wings
and under your gentle feathers I will find refuge.
I will not be afraid when trials and tests are presented.
(Psalms 91)

Yah created man in His own image, in the image of Yah
created He him; male and female created he them.
And Yah blessed them, and Yah said unto them, be fruitful,
and multiply, and replenish the earth, and subdue it.
Genesis 1:27-28

Scriptures for Deliverance

Thou art my hiding place; thou shalt preserve me from trouble; thou shalt compass me about with songs of deliverance. Selah.
Psalms 32:7

The righteous cry, and the Lord heareth, and delivereth them out of all their troubles.The Lord nigh unto them that are of a broken heart; and save such as be of a contrite spirit. Many are the afflictions of the righteous: but the Lord delivers him out of them all.
Psalms 34:17-19

Remember ye not the former things, neither consider the things of old. Behold, I will do a new thing; now it shall spring forth; shall ye not know it? I will even make a way in the wilderness, and rivers in the desert. This people have I formed for myself; they shall shew forth my praise.
Isaiah 43:18-19, 21

The Lord is my rock, and my fortress, and my deliverer; Yah of my rock; in Him will I trust: He is my shield, and the horn of my salvation, my high tower, and my refuge, my Savior; thou saveth me from violence. In my distress I called upon the Lord, and cried to my Yah: and He did hear my voice out of his temple, and my cry did enter into his ears.
2 Samuel 22: 2-3, 7

Scriptures of Healing

I said, Lord, be merciful unto me: heal my soul;
for I have sinned against thee.
Psalms 41:4

Who forgives all thine iniquities; who healeth all thy diseases; who redeemed thy life from destruction; who crowned thee with lovingkindness and tender mercies.
Psalms 103:3-4

The lord is my shepherd; I shall not want.
He restoreth my soul: He leadeth me in the paths of righteousness for his name's sake.
Psalms 23:1, 3

Scriptures regarding the stomach, belly, and the womb

And it cam
e to pass, as she spake these things,
a certain woman of the company lifted up her voice,
and said unto him, Blessed is the womb that bare thee,
and the paps which thou hast sucked.
Luke 11: 27

Lo, children are a heritage of the Lord:
and the fruit of the womb is his reward.
Psalms 127:3

And she spake out with a loud voice, and said, Blessed art
thou among women, and blessed is the fruit of thy womb.
Luke 1:42

Thus saith the Lord that made thee, and formed thee
from the womb, which will help thee.
Isaiah 44:2

Thou hast covered me in my mother's womb.
I will praise thee; for I am fearfully and wonderfully made:
marvelous are thou works; and that my soul knoweth right
well. How precious also are thy thoughts unto me, O Yah!
How great is the sum of them!
Psalms 139:13-14, 17

But thou art he that took me out of the womb: thou didst
make me hope when I was upon my mother's breasts.
I was cast upon thee from the womb:
thou art my God from my mother's belly.
Psalms 22:9-10

His seed (children) shall be mighty upon earth:
the generation of the upright shall be blessed.
Psalms 112:2

Kembo Kembo (Glory Glory)!
Jehovah Rapha is our Healer.
He will take your painful situations
and give them a sweet aroma.
Shalom.

Notes

About the Author

Kasandral Wells was born to Isaiah and Ruthie Wells in the small town of Wynne, Arkansas. She is a graduate of Cross County High School and East Arkansas Community College in Forrest City, Arkansas, where she received an Associate of Arts in Fine Arts. She is a proud mother of two young men, ages 19 and 15 years old. Kasandral enjoys spending time with family and friends, writing, and brainstorming her next creative idea. She is currently on the path to obtaining her Bachelor's Degree in Interdisciplinary Studies at Jonesboro, Arkansas. She is most passionate about being a mother, helping others, being a voice of reason, and pursuing her goals. Kasandral is determined to create her own path and dominate while doing so. She is strong, determined, and more focused than ever before. She is on the path to being the best version of herself.

Also Available from J. Kenkade Publishing

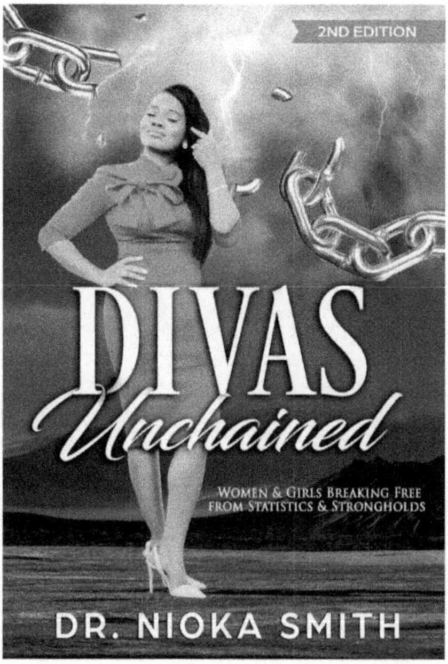

ISBN: 978-1-944486-25-9
Visit www.drniokasmith.com
Author: Dr. Nioka Smith

Sexually abused by her father at the age of 14, pregnant at the age of 17, and a nervous breakdown at the age of 28, Dr. Nioka Smith's painful past almost killed her, until the voice of the Lord guided her into destroying strongholds and reversing Satan's plan for her life. DIVAS Unchained is the powerful chain-breaking reality of the many unfortunate strongholds our women and girls face. Dr. Nioka uses her divine gift to help women and girls break free from destructive life cycles and prosper in all areas of life. Satan has lied to you. It's time to expose his lies. It's time to break free!

Also Available from
J. Kenkade Publishing

ISBN: 978-1-944486-52-5
Visit www.jkenkadepublishing.com
Author: M.A. Howard

"No Matter What, The Past Cannot Change" is one woman's story of abuse, abortion, pregnancy, tragedy, and overcoming adversity to find herself and her voice. M.A. Howard is truly a survivor!

Also Available from J. Kenkade Publishing

ISBN: 978-1-944486-14-3
Visit www.jkenkadepublishing.com
Author: Leakete Jenkins

The story of a young girl born with medical issues and throughout her childhood, suffered molestation, tried to commit suicide, was involved in an abusive relationship, and felt as if no one cared for her. This book will invite you into a story that is so heart-breaking, but will also show you that through any obstacle, God will see you through.

Also Available from J. Kenkade Publishing

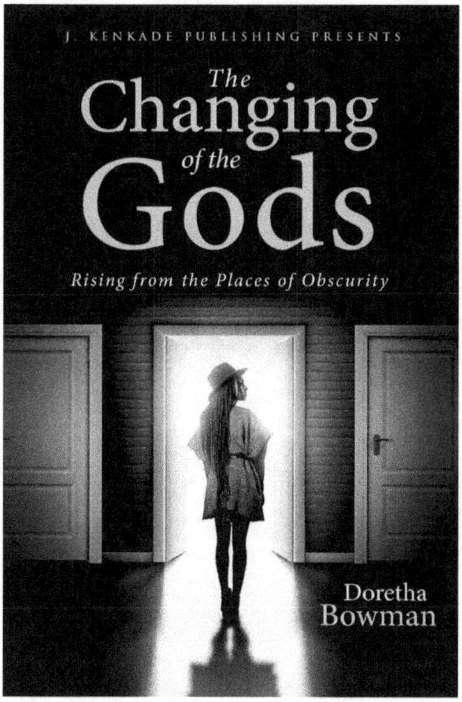

ISBN: 978-1-944486-26-6
Visit www.jkenkadepublishing.com
Author: Doretha Bowman

"The Changing of the Gods" is a personal life story of Doretha Bowman. The book describes her life as it clung to the blind idolization of sin. From drug abuse, alcoholism, and victimization of sexual abuse, Doretha finds a way to make peace with her past through the aid of the guiding light of Christ, the true God. This book allows readers to acknowledge and rise from their places of obscurity to finally find the areas of their life that can be transformed by the light of Jesus Christ's salvation.

Also Available from
J. Kenkade Publishing

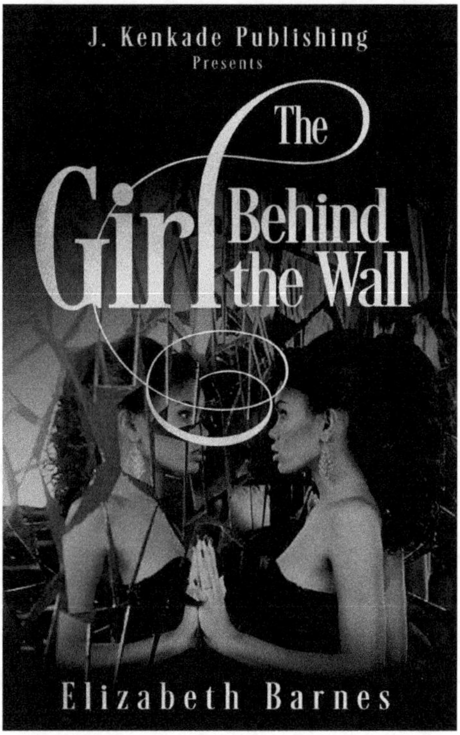

ISBN: 978-1-944486-21-1
Visit www.jkenkadepublishing.com
Author: Elizabeth Barnes

“The Girl Behind the Wall” retells the growing pains of a young woman. She has struggled psychologically from the sexual abuse of family members, pregnancy, mental abuse, and suicidal thoughts. One after another, the devil has tried to keep the growth of Elizabeth hindered. But God said, “No more!

After choosing to turn to God and faith, she has now recovered her life from behind the wall of turmoil the devil created for her.

This page intentionally left blank.
J. Kenkade Publishing

www.ingramcontent.com/pod-product-compliance
Lightning Source LLC
LaVergne TN
LVHW051358080426
835508LV00022B/2872
* 9 7 8 1 9 4 4 4 8 6 5 6 3 *